WORKBOOK

PEARSON EDEXCEL A-LEVEL

Politics  2

GOVERNMENT AND POLITICS OF THE USA AND COMPARATIVE POLITICS

Mark Rathbone

HODDER
EDUCATION
AN HACHETTE UK COMPANY

Although every effort has been made to ensure that website addresses are correct at time of going to press, Hodder Education cannot be held responsible for the content of any website mentioned in this book. It is sometimes possible to find a relocated web page by typing in the address of the home page for a website in the URL window of your browser.

Hachette UK's policy is to use papers that are natural, renewable and recyclable products and made from wood grown in well-managed forests and other controlled sources. The logging and manufacturing processes are expected to conform to the environmental regulations of the country of origin.

Orders: please contact Hachette UK Distribution, Hely Hutchinson Centre, Milton Road, Didcot, Oxfordshire, OX11 7HH. Telephone: +44 (0)1235 827827. Email: education@hachette.co.uk. Lines are open from 9 a.m. to 5 p.m., Monday to Friday. You can also order through our website: www.hoddereducation.co.uk

ISBN: 978 1 3983 3247 8

© Mark Rathbone 2022

First published in 2022 by
Hodder Education,
An Hachette UK Company
Carmelite House
50 Victoria Embankment
London EC4Y 0DZ

www.hoddereducation.co.uk

Impression number   10 9 8 7 6 5 4 3 2 1

Year 2026 2025 2024 2023 2022

Cover photo © Ingo Bartussek – stock.adobe.com

Typeset in India

Printed in India

A catalogue record for this title is available from the British Library.

Contents

About this book

1   This workbook will help you to prepare for the option on Government and Politics of the USA within Component 3 of the Pearson Edexcel A-level Politics (9PL0/3A) exam. This unit focuses on the aspects of US government and politics shown in the chapter headings above. Topic 6 includes work on comparing politics and institutions in the USA with those in the UK, which is how the requirement for synoptic assessment (which requires you to work across different parts of the specification) is met. The knowledge of the UK system of government from your study of Components 1 and 2 will be essential in this comparative element of Component 3.

2   Your exam is 2 hours long and includes a range of 12- and 30-mark questions. The exam is divided into three sections:
    - In Section A you will answer one 12-mark question from a choice of two comparing aspects of UK and US politics.
    - In Section B you will answer a compulsory 12-mark question comparing aspects of UK and US politics, making reference to comparative theories.
    - In Section C you will answer two 30-mark questions from a choice of three on US politics.

3   The questions in this workbook are scaffolded — they begin with easier, lower-mark questions and they work up to more complex questions. Each section ends with questions that are exam-style, encouraging you to think across this and other topics, bringing together all your skills and knowledge.

4   Answering the questions will help you to build your skills and meet the assessment objectives AO1 (knowledge and understanding), AO2 (analysis) and AO3 (evaluation). There is space for you to write your answers.

5   Worked answers are included throughout the practice questions to help you understand how to gain the most marks.

6   Icons next to the question will help you identify:

 where questions draw on synoptic knowledge, i.e. content from more than one topic

 how long this question should take you.

7   You still need to read your textbooks and topic books, and refer to your lesson notes and revision guides. Keeping up to date with US politics by regularly reading news websites is also essential: **theguardian.com**, **www.ft.com/politicsclass**, **washingtonpost.com** and **nytimes.com**, among many others, offer extensive news and analysis of US politics.

8   Marks available are indicated for all questions so that you can gauge the level of detail required in your answers.

9   Timings are given for the exam-style questions to make your practice as realistic as possible. There is space in this workbook for you to write a plan for exam-style questions. Your full answers should then be written on a separate sheet of paper to hand in to your teacher.

10 Answers are available at: **www.hoddereducation.co.uk/workbookanswers**

Topic 1 The US Constitution and federalism

The nature of the US Constitution

The nature of the US Constitution reflects the circumstances under which it was drawn up. In 1776, 13 British colonies in North America, aggrieved by the rule of the monarchy, which they regarded as tyrannical, declared themselves independent. By 1787, however, there was dissatisfaction with the weakness of the central government under the first system of government, the Articles of Confederation, which led to the calling of the Constitutional Convention in Philadelphia.

The Constitution that emerged from this meeting was worded in a vague manner, both to make it acceptable to the differing views of Federalists and Republicans, and to allow some flexibility in how it was interpreted. Its most notable features included codification into a framework allocating different powers to different branches of government, known as separation of powers, and entrenchment, making amendments a complex process requiring supermajorities, as shown in Figure 1.

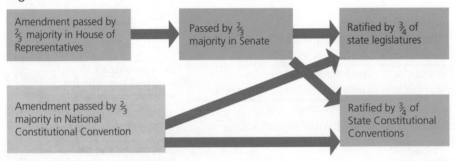

Figure 1 Methods of amending the US Constitution

Practice questions ?

AO1 Knowledge and understanding

1 What were the main differences between the views of Federalists and Republicans at the Constitutional Convention in Philadelphia in 1787? **2 marks**

2 Briefly explain the meaning of the term codification. **2 marks**

3 Briefly explain the meaning of the term entrenchment. **2 marks**

4 Few amendments have been ratified since the Constitution became effective in 1790. Fill in the missing figures in column 2 of the table.

5 marks

Amendment	Figures
Number of constitutional amendments ratified 1790–91 (the Bill of Rights — see Topic 4 for more on this subject)	
Number of constitutional amendments ratified 1792–present	
Passed by two-thirds majority of both Houses of Congress	
Ratified by three-quarters of state legislatures or state constitutional conventions	
Approved by Congress but not so far ratified by enough states	

AO2 Analysis

5 To what extent is the division between Federalists and Republicans still reflected in US politics today?

6 marks

Worked example

The division is reflected in the conflict between liberal Democrats, such as Senators Bernie Sanders and Elizabeth Warren, who argue that the economic and social problems facing the USA require action from a strong central government (for example, Medicare for all), and those, including many Republicans, who believe that the federal government is too powerful and needs to be reduced in both size and spending power.

> AO1 Arguments are supported by specific and up-to-date examples.

> AO2 Argument that the division between Federalists and Republicans is still reflected in US politics today, clearly and concisely explained.

On the other hand, during the presidency of Republican Donald Trump, Democrats frequently protested that he was seeking to increase presidential power at the expense of states. For example, in summer 2020 some Democrat state governors, including Governor Kate Brown (Oregon), criticised President Trump's deployment of federal troops to cities such as Portland, Oregon, during the Black Lives Matter protests. This suggests that disputes regarding state versus federal power, while controversial, are not confined to party lines alone.

> AO2 Counter-argument, again supported by a relevant and recent example.

> AO2 Balanced conclusion.

6 For what reasons has the number of constitutional amendments ratified since 1791 been so limited?

3 marks

....

....

....

....

....

....

7 Choose one of the following:

- Twenty-Fifth Amendment (ratified 1967)
- Twenty-Seventh Amendment (ratified 1992)
- Equal Rights Amendment (originally proposed in 1923; not yet ratified)

Go online to research the amendment you have chosen and explain the issues it concerns and its progress towards ratification.   **5 marks**

....

....

....

....

....

....

....

....

....

....

AO3 Evaluation

8 Evaluate the effectiveness of the formal constitutional amendment process.   **5 marks**

....

....

....

....

....

....

....

....

....

....

....

....

The key features of the US Constitution

Federalism is the principle which divides power between the national government and the state governments (see page 10 for more on this).

The Constitution assigned each of the three branches of government different powers, a principle known as the **separation of powers**, while a system of **checks and balances** gives each branch powers to block actions by the others to prevent one becoming too powerful.

Bipartisanship is the principle that although the parties have different policies and priorities, they are prepared to work with each other and seek agreements through negotiation and compromise.

Limited government is the principle that there are clearly delineated limits to what the government can do, which are spelled out in the Constitution.

Practice questions ?

AO1 Knowledge and understanding

9   Using the table, list the main constitutional powers allocated by the US Constitution to the three branches of government.   14 marks

Executive branch (President)	Legislative branch (Congress)	Judicial branch (Supreme Court)

10 The following are examples of checks and balances. In each case, fill in which branch has the power to do this and which branch is being checked. The first one has been done for you.   10 marks

Branch that has power	Check/balance	Branch whose power is being checked
Executive branch (President)	Veto legislation	Legislative branch (Congress)
	Override veto	
	Strike down Acts of Congress	
	Impeachment	
	Declare executive orders unconstitutional	
	Reject cabinet appointments	

AO2 Analysis

11 Why did the Founding Fathers choose to divide the powers of government between
    three separate branches?   3 marks

....

....

....

....

....

AO3 Evaluation

12 Look up the full text of the Ninth and Tenth Amendments in a textbook or online,
    then evaluate the view that these two amendments make a valuable contribution
    to limiting the power of the US government.   5 marks

....

....

....

....

....

....

....

....

....

....

....

....

....

....

....

The main characteristics of US federalism

Federalism divides power between the national government and the state governments. Yet the Constitution does not define this relationship clearly and does not even mention the words 'federal' or 'federalism'. This has allowed some flexibility in the relationship between the federal government and the states, which has gone through several stages over the past 230 years: **dual federalism** (1791–*c*.1900), **co-operative federalism** (*c*.1900–54), **coercive federalism** (1954–69) and **new federalism** (1969–89).

AO1 Knowledge and understanding

13 Summarise the features of EITHER dual federalism OR coercive federalism.   3 marks

....

....

....

....

AO2 Analysis

14 Explain in your own words the reasons why the US Constitution adopted a federal structure for the government of the USA.   4 marks

....

....

....

....

....

....

15 Explain in your own words the reasons why there was a move away from coercive federalism towards 'new federalism' between 1969 and 1989.   4 marks

....

....

....

....

....

....

....

....

AO3 Evaluation

16 Evaluate the reasons why power transferred from the states to the federal government under presidents George W. Bush and Barack Obama.

6 marks

Worked example

The main reason is that two major national crises required national solutions: the 2001 terrorist attacks and the 2008 financial crisis were too extensive to be dealt with by individual states alone, leading Bush to establish the Department of Homeland Security (after 9/11) and Obama to inject £800 billion into the economy (during the financial crisis). In the case of Bush, this was enhanced by deliberate efforts to increase presidential power, notably the more frequent use of signing statements.

The need for nationally applied standards was an additional reason, for example Bush's No Child Left Behind Act (2001), which obliged schools to conform to federal standards.

All these factors were confirmed by key Supreme Court judgements, which tended to uphold federal government power: ACA Cases (2012) upheld President Obama's healthcare reforms, and *Arizona* v *USA* (2012) affirmed immigration as principally a matter for the federal government.

> **AO3** The most important reason is given in the first sentence.

> **AO2** The answer is developed through analysis of why this factor was crucial in causing power to flow to the federal government.

> **AO1** Factual examples are deployed throughout to support the argument.

> **AO3** A distinction is made between the different reasons under Bush and under Obama.

> **AO3** Secondary reasons are added, establishing a hierarchy of causation.

Interpretations and debates around the US Constitution and federalism

This section draws together many of the arguments about the US Constitution and federalism studied in this chapter, to allow you to evaluate key constitutional debates. Political scientists debate the extent to which the US system of government still fulfils the aims of the Founding Fathers, and they seek to evaluate both the strengths and weaknesses of the US Constitution and its impact on modern US government. Another area of debate is the extent to which the USA remains a truly federal system today. Underlying many of these issues is the key question: How democratic is the USA's system of government?

Practice question ?

AO3 Evaluation

17 Evaluate the view that federalism remains an effective feature of the US system of government today.

5 marks

Copy the table below onto an A4 sheet of paper, enlarging it to fill the whole sheet. In the left-hand column, fill in evidence that federalism remains effective; in the right-hand column, fill in evidence that it is not. In the space at the bottom, write your conclusion as to whether, on balance, federalism remains effective or not.

Evidence that federalism remains effective	Evidence that federalism is ineffective
Conclusion:	

Paper 3 Section C

All of these exam-style questions require you to demonstrate AO1 (knowledge and understanding), AO2 (analysis) and AO3 (evaluation) in your answers.

1   Evaluate the extent to which the efforts of the Founding Fathers to set limits on federal government power are still effective. You must consider this view and the alternative to this view in a balanced way.

30 marks

Write a plan here, then use a separate sheet of paper to answer the question in full.

....
....
....
....
....
....

2   Evaluate the view that the separation of powers is a recipe for gridlock and weak government in the USA. You must consider this view and the alternative to this view in a balanced way.

30 marks

Write a plan here, then use a separate sheet of paper to answer the question in full.

....
....
....
....
....
....

3   Evaluate the view that checks and balances between the three branches of the federal government work effectively. You must consider this view and the alternative to this view in a balanced way.

30 marks

Write a plan here, then use a separate sheet of paper to answer the question in full.

....
....
....
....
....
....

4   Evaluate the extent to which bipartisanship still exists in the US system of government today. You must consider this view and the alternative to this view in a balanced way.

30 marks

Write a plan here, then use a separate sheet of paper to answer the question in full.

40

....

....

....

....

....

....

....

5   Evaluate the extent to which the USA's system of government is democratic. You must consider this view and the alternative to this view in a balanced way.

30 marks

Write a plan here, then use a separate sheet of paper to answer the question in full.

40

....

....

....

....

....

....

....

6   Evaluate the view that the US Constitution is outdated and ineffective. You must consider this view and the alternative to this view in a balanced way.

30 marks

Write a plan here, then use a separate sheet of paper to answer the question in full.

40

....

....

....

....

....

....

....

Topic 2 The US Congress

The structure of Congress

Article I of the US Constitution specifies that Congress shall be bicameral, consisting of the Senate and the House of Representatives, each elected by different methods and for different terms. Article I also states that Congress has 'all legislative powers' and goes on to mention a number of specific powers, listed in Question 2 below. Some of these are exclusive powers given to one house, but not the other, while others are 'concurrent powers', exercised together by Congress as a whole.

Practice questions ?

AO1 Knowledge and understanding

1   The US Constitution specifies that the House and the Senate are elected by different methods and for different terms. Fill in the details in the following table.   **12 marks**

House	Allocation of seats to states	Electorate	Length of terms
House of Representatives			
Senate			

2   For each of the selected powers listed below, say whether they are exercised by the House of Representatives, by the Senate or by both concurrently.   **12 marks**

Power	Exercised by the House of Representatives, by the Senate or by both concurrently
To make laws	
To originate finance bills	
To give 'advice and consent' to treaties	
To regulate interstate commerce	
To pass articles of impeachment	
To hold impeachment trials	
To ratify appointments	

3 Summarise the House of Representatives' constitutional authority to originate spending bills.

3 marks

....

....

....

....

....

AO2 Analysis

4 Answer the following questions about the provisions of Article I for Congress.

   a Why was the number of representatives proportional to the population of each state, whereas the number of senators was a fixed number per state, regardless of size?

2 marks

....

....

....

   b Why did the Constitution originally specify that the senators from each state should be chosen by the state legislature, rather than being elected?

2 marks

....

....

....

   c Why did Sections 2 and 3 provide for different election intervals for the House of Representatives and the Senate?

2 marks

....

....

....

5 State three advantages of a bicameral structure for a legislature.

3 marks

....

....

....

....

....

6   State three disadvantages of a bicameral structure for a legislature.   3 marks

....

....

....

....

....

....

7   How democratic is the US Senate?   6 marks

....

....

....

....

....

....

....

....

....

....

....

....

....

....

The functions of Congress

The principal functions of Congress are **representative** (reflecting accurately the views of the people), **legislative** (enacting laws for the good of the people) and **oversight** (checking the executive branch, to ensure effective and fair governance). Each of these functions raises several issues: the fairness of elections and factors affecting voting behaviour in Congress (such as caucuses and pressure groups), the impact and effectiveness of the legislative process (including committees), and the effectiveness of congressional oversight of the president.

AO1 Knowledge and understanding

8   The committee system is central to the legislative progress. Complete the table, explaining the nature and functions of different types of congressional committee.   8 marks

Type of committee	Nature and functions
Standing committees	
Select committees	
Conference committees	

9   The following are examples of congressional caucuses (groupings of congress(wo)men with something in common who meet periodically to further legislative objectives). In each case, research and summarise the aims and membership of the caucus.

a   Blue Dog Coalition   2 marks

....

....

....

....

b   Congressional Black Caucus   2 marks

....

....

....

....

c   Congressional Caucus on International Exchange and Study   2 marks

....

....

....

....

10 Summarise the operation of the filibuster in the Senate and how the rules governing its use have changed significantly in recent years.

4 marks

Worked example

In the Senate, minority party members can block a bill by use of the filibuster — making lengthy speeches to indefinitely delay the bill's progress (although today it is usually only necessary to declare the intention to do so). A filibuster can only be broken by a cloture motion (a decision to end debate and move to a vote), which requires the support of 60 out of 100 senators. Following rule changes in 2013 and 2017, the filibuster was eliminated for votes on presidential appointments, including, from 2017, Supreme Court justices. There is no equivalent to the filibuster in the House of Representatives.

AO1 Defines terminology clearly and concisely at the start.

AO1 Follows up with significant factual details.

AO1 As the second part of the question calls for, explains the effects of recent rule changes.

AO1 Draws distinction between the Senate and the House of Representatives.

AO2 Analysis

Analysis of 2020 congressional election results: the 'incumbency advantage'			
House	Number of incumbents seeking re-election	Number re-elected	Percentage re-elected
House of Representatives	407	372	91%
Senate	31	26	84%

11 Study the figures in the table above. Why does incumbency confer such a great advantage in congressional elections?

4 marks

....

....

....

....

....

....

....

....

12 Pressure groups and lobbyists can be a major influence on Congress. Explain why the National Rifle Association (NRA) is particularly powerful.

3 marks

....

....

....

....

....

4 marks

13 What is meant by 'pork-barrelling' and why is it often considered unethical? 3 marks

....

....

....

....

....

....

14 Explain why the Senate Judiciary Committee is particularly important. 2 marks

....

....

....

....

AO3 Evaluation

15 To what extent does redistricting make Congress less representative? 5 marks

Worked example

In states in which redistricting is done by the state legislature, the party in control of the legislature determines the electoral boundaries for the next 10 years. They sometimes do so in a way that benefits their own party's electoral prospects, a process known as 'gerrymandering'. It is argued that reinforcing one-party dominance in a seat means that fewer seats in the House of Representatives are truly competitive. There is a consistently higher incumbency re-election rate for House elections than for elections to the Senate — 91% and 84% respectively in 2020. This supports the contention that redistricting makes the House less representative.

AO2 Analyses with clarity how redistricting works.

AO2 Explains argument that it does make Congress less representative.

AO3 Evaluates this argument using a statistical example.

On the other hand, there are limits to these effects. In a few states, such as Iowa, redistricting is determined by a non-partisan commission, and smaller states, such as Wyoming, have only one seat in the House of Representatives, so redistricting does not arise. Also, the Senate, whose members are elected to represent a state, not a district, is unaffected by redistricting.

AO3 Presents a counter-argument, well supported by factual examples.

Overall, there is real cause for concern that redistricting does make the House less representative, a judgement which is borne out by Supreme Court cases requiring some states to redraw electoral maps, such as *Wittman* v *Personhuballah* (2016) and *Cooper* v *Harris* (2017).

AO3 Reaches a substantiated, reasoned judgement on the question.

Interpretations and debates around Congress

This section draws together many of the key debates about the role of Congress, which we have already touched on in this chapter. Current areas of debate include the extent to which the relative importance of different roles and powers of Congress has changed in recent years. An increase in partisanship and polarisation of political opinion has been evident in many areas of US politics in the past three decades, and arguably Congress has been affected by this more than any other institution, as evidenced by a decline in the number of centrists elected in both parties and an increase in the number of party-line votes.

The effectiveness of Congress in performing its representative and legislative roles, and in holding the presidency to account, continues to be under scrutiny, leading to the perennial question of whether it is a fair assessment to dismiss Congress as 'the broken branch'.

Practice questions **?**

AO3 Evaluation

16 To what extent can it be argued that when a president faces one or both Houses of Congress controlled by the other party, Congress can become overly critical of the president in a way which is negative and destructive? **6 marks**

17 To what extent can it be argued that at times, when the same party controls the presidency and both Houses of Congress, congressional oversight of the executive is neglected, and the legislative branch becomes too much the lapdog of the president? **4 marks**

....

....

....

....

....

....

....

....

Exam-style questions ?

Paper 3 Section C

All of these exam-style questions require you to demonstrate AO1 (knowledge and understanding), AO2 (analysis) and AO3 (evaluation) in your answers.

1 Evaluate the view that the legislative process in Congress works effectively. You must consider this view and the alternative to this view in a balanced way. **30 marks**

Write a plan here, then use a separate sheet of paper to answer the question in full.

40

....

....

....

....

....

2 Evaluate the view that the Senate is more powerful than the House of Representatives. You must consider this view and the alternative to this view in a balanced way. **30 marks**

Write a plan here, then use a separate sheet of paper to answer the question in full.

40

....

....

....

....

3 Evaluate the extent to which incumbents have an advantage over challengers in congressional elections. You must consider this view and the alternative to this view in a balanced way.

30 marks

40

Write a plan here, then use a separate sheet of paper to answer the question in full.

....

....

....

....

....

....

4 Evaluate the view that Congress does not accurately represent the American people. You must consider this view and the alternative to this view in a balanced way.

30 marks

40

Write a plan here, then use a separate sheet of paper to answer the question in full.

....

....

....

....

....

....

5 Evaluate the extent to which the role of parties in Congress has changed over the past three decades. You must consider this view and the alternative to this view in a balanced way.

30 marks

40

Write a plan here, then use a separate sheet of paper to answer the question in full.

....

....

....

....

....

....

6   Evaluate the extent to which Congress has a meaningful role in foreign policy.
     You must consider this view and the alternative to this view in a balanced way.   **30 marks**   40

Write a plan here, then use a separate sheet of paper to answer the question in full.

....

....

....

....

....

....

....

7   Evaluate the extent to which Congress is able to check the executive branch
     effectively. You must consider this view and the alternative to this view in a
     balanced way.   **30 marks**   40

Write a plan here, then use a separate sheet of paper to answer the question in full.

....

....

....

....

....

....

....

8   Evaluate the view that Congress can fairly be considered to be 'the broken
     branch'. You must consider this view and the alternative to this view in a
     balanced way.   **30 marks**   40

Write a plan here, then use a separate sheet of paper to answer the question in full.

....

....

....

....

....

....

....

Topic 3 The US presidency

Formal sources of presidential power as outlined in the US Constitution and their use

The US presidency embodies a dual role as head of state and as head of government — in President Theodore Roosevelt's words, 'almost that of a king and a prime minister rolled into one'.

The formal powers of the presidency are spelt out in Articles I and II of the Constitution:

Article I   To veto legislation

Article II   To be 'commander in chief of the Army and Navy of the United States'

        To 'grant reprieves and pardons'

        To 'make treaties'

        To 'appoint ambassadors, other public ministers and consuls'

        To nominate 'judges of the Supreme Court'

        To nominate 'all other officers of the United States'

        To 'from time to time give to the Congress information of the state of the union'

        To recommend to Congress legislation 'as he shall judge necessary and expedient'

        To summon special sessions of Congress 'on extraordinary occasions'

        To 'take care that the laws be faithfully executed'

Practice questions ?

AO1 Knowledge and understanding

1 Enter the 11 formal powers of the president named above in the Venn diagram below, according to whether they are part of the role of head of state or that of head of government, or effectively of both.

6 marks

Head of State   Head of Government

Figure 2 The presidential roles of head of state and head of government

AO2 Analysis

2   For each of the three formal powers listed below, give one example since 1992 of a president using that power and explain the significance of that use.

   a   To be 'commander in chief of the Army and Navy of the United States'   4 marks

....

....

....

....

....

....

....

   b   To veto legislation   4 marks

....

....

....

....

....

....

....

   c   To 'grant reprieves and pardons'   4 marks

....

....

....

....

....

....

....

3 Evaluate the validity of Theodore Roosevelt's summary of the US president's role as 'almost that of a king and a prime minister rolled into one'.

6 marks

....

....

....

....

....

....

....

....

....

....

....

....

....

....

....

....

....

....

Informal sources of presidential power and their use

Some presidents are more powerful than others due to a variety of factors, or 'informal powers', which vary from one president to another, either enhancing or diminishing a president's authority. These include the size of their electoral mandate, their use of executive orders, the consequences of national events, their cabinet, their personal character and powers of persuasion, and their use of the Executive Office of the President (EXOP) and other executive branch agencies.

AO1 Knowledge and understanding

4 Summarise the role of the Executive Office of the President (EXOP). *3 marks*

....

....

....

....

....

....

5 Summarise the role of the Office of Management and Budget (OMB). *3 marks*

....

....

....

....

....

....

AO2 Analysis

6 What is the constitutional justification for executive orders and why are they sometimes controversial? *5 marks*

Worked example

Executive orders are not specifically mentioned in the Constitution. However, they are justified by the president's constitutional power to 'take care that the laws be faithfully executed' and, despite some restrictions on their use, they have the full force of law.

> AO1 Clearly states the constitutional basis for executive orders at the start, quoting the relevant phrase from the Constitution.

They can become controversial for several reasons:

> AO2 Moves on to the analytical part of the question, clearly explaining three reasons why executive orders can be controversial.

1   When they are used very frequently, e.g. President Bill Clinton issued 364 executive orders, more than any subsequent president.

2   When they represent an attempt to by-pass Congress, e.g. President Trump's Executive Order 13813, which tried effectively to replace the Affordable Care Act in October 2017 after he had failed to persuade Congress to repeal it.

> AO1 In each case, provides factual examples to support the argument.

3   When executive orders are used to address highly contentious issues, e.g. in April 2021, President Biden used Executive Order 14023 to establish the Presidential Commission on the Supreme Court of the United States, seen by some commentators as a first step towards expansion of the court to more than nine justices.

7 **a** Discuss the effects of the 2008 financial crisis on Obama's presidency.   **4 marks**

....

....

....

....

....

....

....

b Discuss the effects of the Covid-19 pandemic during 2020 on the presidency of Donald Trump.   **4 marks**

....

....

....

....

....

....

....

8 What qualities does a president look for when choosing cabinet members? Give examples from at least two presidents to illustrate your answer.   **5 marks**

....

....

....

....

....

....

....

....

....

AO3 Evaluation

9   In 1960, the political scientist Richard Neustadt wrote that the foremost power of the
US president is 'the power to persuade'. Evaluate the importance of a president's
communication skills, with examples from presidents since 1992.   **5 marks**

Worked example

The separation of powers means that presidents cannot merely
issue orders, but must persuade others, principally Congress,
to back their policies. Presidents' communication skills are
therefore crucial to how powerful they can be. A populist
ability to connect with the public enhances a president's
power and can help to overcome difficulties. For example,
though often dismissed as inarticulate, **George W. Bush** was
able to communicate effectively with ordinary voters, notably
after the 9/11 terrorist attacks. **Barack Obama**'s fluency and
eloquence as a public speaker brought him to national attention
in 2004 and remained a significant factor in the success of
his presidency. **Donald Trump** used Twitter extensively to
communicate his ideas directly to the public and to attack his
perceived enemies.

On the other hand, the president has other, more formal
powers, such as the power to nominate Supreme Court
justices, the position as commander-in-chief and the power of
veto. It could be argued that these are of greater significance
than the informal 'power to persuade'.

Overall, as the examples cited show, the ability to persuade
remains crucial to presidential success, although the means of
communication available have changed enormously since 1960.

> AO2 Clear analysis of a major constitutional principle.

> AO3 Develops argument, evaluating the importance of the president's communication skills.

> AO2 Provides examples from three successive presidencies, not only demonstrating good knowledge but using it selectively to support the argument with varied factual evidence.

> AO3 Produces well-supported counter-argument.

> AO3 Reaches a substantiated reasoned judgement on the question.

10 Evaluate the importance of winning the popular vote to a president's strength
in office.   **5 marks**

The presidency

There is often tension between the presidency and the other two branches of government, which at times resembles a struggle for supremacy. This is exacerbated when Congress is controlled by one party and the presidency by another, but even when the same party controls both branches, as from 2017 to 2019, that is no guarantee of consistently good relations between them. Supreme Court judgements can also restrict a president's freedom of action, and the power a president wields can vary at different times during their term in office.

AO1 Knowledge and understanding

11 Research the following events:
- President George W. Bush's use of signing statements
- President Obama's response to *Citizens United* v *FEC* in January 2010
- President Trump and the 2019 Budget

For each, summarise briefly below what happened and what the event tells us about relations between the presidency and the other two branches.

a Bush and signing statements   4 marks

....
....
....
....
....
....
....

b Obama and *Citizens United*   4 marks

....
....
....
....
....
....
....

c   Trump and the 2019 Budget   4 marks

....

....

....

....

....

....

....

AO2 Analysis

12 Complete the table, explaining the effects of three factors on presidential power
   and citing examples demonstrated by the different presidents who held
   office between 1993 and 2021.   16 marks

Factor	Effects this factor may have on a president's power	Example, since 1993
Congress		
The election cycle and divided government		
Supreme Court		

AO3 Evaluation

13 Evaluate the relative significance of the three factors mentioned in the table in
Question 12 in determining how powerful a president is in practice.   **4 marks**

....

....

....

....

....

....

....

....

Interpretations and debates of the US presidency

In considering key debates about the presidency, the specification requires you
to refer to presidents since 1993 — Bill Clinton, George W. Bush, Barack Obama,
Donald Trump and Joe Biden.

The Imperial Presidency is the title of a 1973 book by Arthur M. Schlesinger
Jr. about the growth and misuse of presidential power, and the term has been
revived in discussions relating to the twenty-first century presidency. Analysing
how effectively recent presidents have achieved their aims, considering whether
Congress can in practice hold presidents accountable and assessing the extent
to which presidents dominate foreign policy are all facets of this complex debate
about presidential power.

Practice question ?

AO3 Evaluation

14 Can Trump be considered an 'imperial president'?   **5 marks**
*Copy the table below onto A4 paper, enlarging it to fill the whole sheet. In the left-hand
column, fill in evidence that Trump was an 'imperial president'; in the right-hand column, fill in
evidence that he was a weak president. In the space at the bottom, write your conclusion as
to whether on balance he can be considered an 'imperial president' or not.*

Evidence that Trump was an 'imperial president'	Evidence that Trump was not an 'imperial president'
Conclusion:	

Paper 3 Section C

All of these exam-style questions require you to demonstrate AO1 (knowledge and understanding), AO2 (analysis) and AO3 (evaluation) in your answers.

1   Evaluate the extent to which Obama achieved his aims as president. You must consider this view and the alternative to this view in a balanced way.   **30 marks**

Write a plan here, then use a separate sheet of paper to answer the question in full.

40

....

....

....

....

....

....

2   Evaluate the view that the power of the president is greatly affected by the strength of their electoral mandate. You must consider this view and the alternative to this view in a balanced way.   **30 marks**

Write a plan here, then use a separate sheet of paper to answer the question in full.

40

....

....

....

....

....

....

3   Evaluate the view that a president's power inevitably declines during a second term in office. You must consider this view and the alternative to this view in a balanced way.   **30 marks**

Write a plan here, then use a separate sheet of paper to answer the question in full.

40

....

....

....

....

....

....

4 Evaluate the view that the roles of the Executive Office of the President and the cabinet are highly significant in the executive branch. You must consider this view and the alternative to this view in a balanced way.

30 marks

Write a plan here, then use a separate sheet of paper to answer the question in full.

....

....

....

....

....

....

....

5 Evaluate the view that the president's veto powers have caused conflict between the legislative and executive branches. You must consider this view and the alternative to this view in a balanced way.

30 marks

Write a plan here, then use a separate sheet of paper to answer the question in full.

....

....

....

....

....

....

....

6 Evaluate the extent to which the president has influence over the legislative process. You must consider this view and the alternative to this view in a balanced way.

30 marks

Write a plan here, then use a separate sheet of paper to answer the question in full.

....

....

....

....

....

....

....

7   Evaluate the extent to which the label 'imperial presidency' is an appropriate
    description of the executive branch in the twenty-first century. You must consider
    this view and the alternative to this view in a balanced way.   **30 marks**

    Write a plan here, then use a separate sheet of paper to answer the question in full.

....

....

....

....

....

....

....

8   Evaluate the view that the power of impeachment is a powerful check on the
    presidency. You must consider this view and the alternative to this view in a
    balanced way.   **30 marks**

    Write a plan here, then use a separate sheet of paper to answer the question in full.

....

....

....

....

....

....

....

....

9   Evaluate the view that the checks on the president's powers over defence and
    foreign policy are ineffective. You must consider this view and the alternative
    to this view in a balanced way.   **30 marks**

    Write a plan here, then use a separate sheet of paper to answer the question in full.

....

....

....

....

....

....

Topic 4 The US Supreme Court and civil rights

The nature and role of the Supreme Court

Article III of the US Constitution allocates judicial power to the US Supreme Court, and the separation of powers gives it independence to act as a referee, upholding the Constitution. With power to strike down Acts of Congress, decisions of the executive branch and state laws, the Supreme Court ensures that all the other branches act constitutionally, exercising this power through the process of judicial review.

Practice questions ?

AO1 Knowledge and understanding

1 The official text of the US Constitution can be found on this US government website: **www.archives.gov/exhibits/charters/constitution_transcript.html**. In your own words, summarise Article III, Sections 1 and 2, which explain the powers of the Supreme Court.

4 marks

....

....

....

....

....

....

2 What is meant by judicial review?

2 marks

....

....

....

AO2 Analysis

3 Explain how the Constitution safeguards the independence of the Supreme Court.

4 marks

....

....

....

....

....

4 Explain the significance of Federalist Paper No. 78, published in 1788, to the powers of the Supreme Court.

3 marks

....

....

....

....

....

AO3 Evaluation

5 How significant is the Supreme Court's power of judicial review?

5 marks

....

....

....

....

....

....

....

....

....

....

....

....

....

The appointment process for the Supreme Court

Nominated by the president when a vacancy occurs

Rated for qualification to serve by the American Bar Association (ABA)

Publicly questioned at length and then voted on by the Senate Judicial Committee

Debated and voted on by the whole Senate

Figure 3 The appointment process for US Supreme Court justices

AO1 Knowledge and understanding

6 Fill in the missing information in the table showing the nomination process of selected recent nominees for the Supreme Court.

10 marks

Nominee	Year	Nominating president	ABA rating	Judicial Committee vote	Senate vote
Robert Bork	1987	Reagan (R)	Well qualified	5–9 against	Rejected 42–58
Ruth Bader Ginsburg	1993	Clinton (D)	Well qualified	18–0 for	
Harriet Miers	2005	George W. Bush (R)	Questionable		
Samuel Alito	2006	George W. Bush (R)	Qualified	10–8 for	
Sonia Sotomayor	2009		Well qualified	18–0 for	
Merrick Garland	2016	Obama (D)	Well qualified		
Neil Gorsuch	2017		Well qualified	11–9 for	
Brett Kavanaugh	2018	Trump (R)	Well qualified	11–10 for	
Amy Coney Barrett	2020	Trump (R)	Well qualified	12–0 for	

7 What is meant by a 'swing justice'?

2 marks

....

....

....

....

AO2 Analysis

8 Explain why those who wrote the Constitution made the process by which justices are appointed to the Supreme Court so complex.

4 marks

....

....

....

....

....

....

....

9 Choose two of the following nominees for the Supreme Court: Robert Bork, Clarence Thomas, Harriet Miers, Elena Kagan, Neil Gorsuch, Amy Coney Barrett. Explain why their nominations and hearings were controversial.   **6 marks**

....

....

....

....

....

....

....

....

....

....

....

....

....

....

....

....

....

10 Explain why the appointment process of Supreme Court justices has become increasingly politicised in recent years.   **3 marks**

Worked example

The appointment process has become more politicised since 2005 due to the general polarisation of US politics, the fine balance between liberal and conservative justices on the Court and the likely length of service of justices. President Trump's appointments, Neil Gorsuch (2017), Brett Kavanaugh (2018) and Amy Coney Barrett (2020), may still be on the Supreme Court in the 2040s. These three appointments were especially controversial because the filibuster rules were changed to force through the confirmation of Gorsuch, Kavanaugh was confirmed despite an accusation of sexual assault made against him, and Barrett's confirmation was rushed through just 8 days before an election.

> **AO2** Gets straight to the point, listing three major causes of politicisation in the first sentence.

> **AO1** Develops and supports the third of these points with up-to-date information.

> **AO1** Provides detail of specific recent examples.

Topic 4 The US Supreme Court and civil rights

11 Explain why the four factors given below are important considerations for a president choosing a nominee for the Supreme Court. **10 marks**

a   the nominee's judicial experience

b   whether their judicial outlook is conservative or liberal

c   how their appointment would affect the current balance on the Court

d   whether they are likely to be approved by the Senate

....

....

....

....

....

....

....

....

....

....

....

AO3 Evaluation

12 Evaluate the reasons why the Republicans in the Senate blocked President Obama's nomination of Merrick Garland in 2016, and the grounds on which this was criticised by Democrats. **5 marks**

....

....

....

....

....

....

....

....

....

....

....

....

The Supreme Court and public policy

The Supreme Court's decisions often have political implications and can have a major effect on public policy in a variety of areas. When the Supreme Court makes only cautious and infrequent use of the power of judicial review, this is referred to as 'judicial restraint'. Since the era of Chief Justice Earl Warren (1953–69), however, the Court has made frequent use of its power to strike down federal or state laws in a significant number of landmark cases affecting many aspects of public policy.

Practice questions ❓

AO1 Knowledge and understanding

13 What is meant by *stare decisis*?   2 marks

....

....

14 What is meant by judicial activism?   3 marks

....

....

....

AO2 Analysis

15 For each of the cases in the table, summarise the Supreme Court's decision and analyse its implications for the area of public policy named.

Go online to research them: **www.scotusblog.com**, **www.law.cornell.edu** and **www.oyez.org** are useful websites.   3 marks for each

Case	Supreme Court's decision and implications for named public policy
Harris Funeral Homes v *Equal Employment Opportunity Commission* (2020) (transgender rights)	
Fisher v *University of Texas* (2016) (affirmative action)	
Tandon v *Newsom* (2021) (religious freedom)	
Sessions v *Dimaya* (2018) (rights of immigrants)	
McCutcheon v *FEC* (2014) (campaign funding)	

AO3 Evaluation

16 Evaluate the significance of the Supreme Court's rulings on abortion.   5 marks

....
....
....
....
....
....
....
....
....
....
....
....

17 Research the case *Citizens United* v *FEC* (2010). Evaluate the extent to which the
Roberts Court can fairly be accused of judicial activism in its decision in this case.   5 marks

....
....
....
....
....
....
....
....
....
....
....
....

The protection of civil liberties and rights in the USA today

Some rights are specifically protected by the US Constitution. For example, Article I, Section 9 mentions three significant individual rights: 'The privilege of the Writ of Habeas Corpus shall not be suspended, unless when in Cases of Rebellion or Invasion the public Safety may require it. No Bill of Attainder or ex post facto Law shall be passed.' The Bill of Rights, ratified in 1791, codified other rights of US citizens. Since then, 17 further amendments have been ratified, some of which have established significant additional rights.

The Supreme Court often acts to protect the rights of citizens, and its rulings can sometimes effectively create additional rights by reinterpreting the Constitution in such a way as to recognise rights which had not been accepted previously, as in *Harris Funeral Homes* v *Equal Employment Opportunity Commission* (2020).

Practice questions

AO1 Knowledge and understanding

18 Summarise the meaning and importance of the following terms.   **6 marks**

Term	Meaning/importance
Habeas corpus	
Bill of attainder	
Ex post facto law	

19 The table shows selected rights guaranteed by the Bill of Rights (the first ten amendments). Summarise the rights covered by each of the amendments cited; the First Amendment has been done for you.   **6 marks**

Amendment	Rights
First	No established religion; freedoms of religion, speech and assembly; right to petition
Second	
Fifth	
Sixth	
Eighth	
Ninth	
Tenth	

AO2 Analysis

20 Choose two of the following amendments and discuss modern controversies
about their interpretation:
- First Amendment • Second Amendment • Eighth Amendment   8 marks

....

....

....

....

....

....

....

....

....

....

....

....

....

21 Research the Twenty-Sixth Amendment, explaining how it added to the rights of
US citizens.   4 marks

....

....

....

....

....

....

....

....

22 Research the case *Peña Rodriguez* v *Colorado* (2017), explaining how it protected
   a constitutional right of US citizens.   4 marks

....

....

....

....

....

23 Research the case *Obergefell* v *Hodges* (2015), explaining how it added to the
   rights of US citizens.   4 marks

....

....

....

....

....

AO3 Evaluation

24 How effectively did the US Supreme Court protect the rights of US citizens in its
   judgement in the case *Foster* v *Chatman* (2016)?   5 marks

Worked example

The Court ruled 7–1 that Timothy Foster, a black American
sentenced to death for murder in Georgia in 1987 and on death
row ever since, had not received a fair trial because state
officials had systematically and illegally excluded black people
from the jury. 'The focus on race in the prosecution's file plainly
demonstrates a concerted effort to keep black prospective
jurors off the jury,' Chief Justice Roberts wrote.

> AO1 Clear factual summary of the case.

The fact that such blatant racial discrimination could still take
place seemed a disturbing throwback to the bad old days of
the Deep South in the 1950s, and the Supreme Court rightly
acted to declare the trial invalid and overturn the verdict.
On the other hand, this case did not reach the Supreme Court
until 29 years after the original trial, during which time the
accused was imprisoned on death row — a very long time for
Foster to wait in jail for recognition that his right to a fair trial
had been violated, making the Court's protection of his rights
less effective.

> AO3 Develops argument, evaluating the Supreme Court's response positively.

> AO3 Provides a counter-argument, suggesting that the protection of rights was not so effective.

Nevertheless, the case set a precedent that should help to
ensure this injustice doesn't happen again, therefore protecting
the rights of all US citizens.

> AO3 Reaches a reasoned judgement.

Race and rights in contemporary US politics

The Civil Rights Act (1964) and the Voting Rights Act (1965) represented a triumph for the non-violent campaigning of the civil rights movement. The election of the USA's first black president, Barack Obama, in 2008, was also rightly seen as a milestone of great significance. Yet black and Hispanic people remain on average poorer, less well-educated, underrepresented and more likely to be targeted by police violence than white Americans, as attested by the deaths in 2020 of Breonna Taylor and George Floyd, both of whom were killed by police officers. Today, campaigning by civil rights organisations focuses on issues such as voting rights, affirmative action, poverty and policing.

Practice questions ?

AO1 Knowledge and understanding

25 What did the Civil Rights Act (1964) achieve for black Americans?   2 marks

....

....

....

....

26 What did the Voting Rights Act (1965) achieve for black Americans?   2 marks

....

....

....

....

27 What is meant by affirmative action?   2 marks

....

....

....

....

AO2 Analysis

28 Why are voter ID laws opposed by civil rights organisations?   3 marks

....

....

....

....

....

29 Research the work of one of the following civil rights organisations today:

- National Association for the Advancement of Colored People (NAACP)
- By Any Means Necessary (BAMN)
- Black Lives Matter (BLM)

Analyse the aims and campaigning methods of your chosen organisation.   **4 marks**

....
....
....
....
....
....
....
....
....
....

30 Why do a substantial majority of black people vote for the Democratic Party?   **5 marks**

....
....
....
....
....
....
....
....
....
....
....
....
....

31 Evaluate the extent to which the American Civil Liberties Union (ACLU) has successfully protected the rights of US citizens.

5 marks

....

....

....

....

....

....

....

....

....

....

....

....

....

....

....

....

....

....

....

Interpretations and debates of the US Supreme Court

Since *Marbury* v *Madison* in 1803, the relationship between the Court and the Constitution has proved controversial. Debates focus on whether the Court has become too political, the judicial philosophy of its justices, how effectively it upholds the rights of the people, and whether 'judicial supremacy' has upset the constitutional balance between the three branches of government. The controversy generated by Senate Republicans blocking President Obama's nominee in 2016, only to rush through President Trump's nominee, Amy Coney Barrett, in 2020, has further heightened concerns about extreme politicisation of the Supreme Court.

AO3 Evaluation

32 Evaluate the significance of the differences between 'living constitution' ideology and originalism.

5 marks

....

....

....

....

....

....

....

....

....

....

....

....

....

Paper 3 Section C

All of these exam-style questions require you to demonstrate AO1 (knowledge and understanding), AO2 (analysis) and AO3 (evaluation) in your answers.

1 Evaluate the extent to which the Supreme Court's power of judicial review is controversial. You must consider this view and the alternative to this view in a balanced way.

30 marks

Write a plan here, then use a separate sheet of paper to answer the question in full.

40

....

....

....

....

....

....

....

....

....

2   Evaluate the view that the appointment process to the Supreme Court is no
    longer fit for purpose. You must consider this view and the alternative to
    this view in a balanced way.   **30 marks**

    Write a plan here, then use a separate sheet of paper to answer the question in full.

    ....

    ....

    ....

    ....

    ....

    ....

3   Evaluate the view that the main reason why appointments to the US Supreme
    Court have become increasingly politically controversial since 1993 is the general
    polarisation of US politics. You must consider this view and the alternative to this
    view in a balanced way.   **30 marks**

    Write a plan here, then use a separate sheet of paper to answer the question in full.

    ....

    ....

    ....

    ....

    ....

    ....

    ....

4   Evaluate the extent to which the Supreme Court has been influential on public
    policy in recent years. You must consider this view and the alternative to this
    view in a balanced way.   **30 marks**

    Write a plan here, then use a separate sheet of paper to answer the question in full.

    ....

    ....

    ....

    ....

    ....

    ....

5   Evaluate the extent to which the US Supreme Court has protected the
    constitutional rights of citizens in recent years. You must consider this view
    and the alternative to this view in a balanced way.   **30 marks**   40

Write a plan here, then use a separate sheet of paper to answer the question in full.

....

....

....

....

....

....

....

6   Evaluate the extent to which campaigns to defend affirmative action have met with
    success in recent years. You must consider this view and the alternative to this
    view in a balanced way.   **30 marks**   40

Write a plan here, then use a separate sheet of paper to answer the question in full.

....

....

....

....

....

....

....

7   Evaluate the view that racial problems remain a major issue in US politics.
    You must consider this view and the alternative to this view in a balanced way.   **30 marks**   40

Write a plan here, then use a separate sheet of paper to answer the question in full.

....

....

....

....

....

....

....

8 Evaluate the view that the Supreme Court has become excessively political in recent years, to the detriment of its judicial function. You must consider this view and the alternative to this view in a balanced way.

30 marks

40

Write a plan here, then use a separate sheet of paper to answer the question in full.

....

....

....

....

....

....

....

....

9 Evaluate the extent to which the Supreme Court is independent of the other branches of government. You must consider this view and the alternative to this view in a balanced way.

30 marks

40

Write a plan here, then use a separate sheet of paper to answer the question in full.

....

....

....

....

....

....

....

10 Evaluate the view that Congress is more powerful than the US Supreme Court. You must consider this view and the alternative to this view in a balanced way.

30 marks

40

Write a plan here, then use a separate sheet of paper to answer the question in full.

....

....

....

....

....

....

Topic 5 US democracy and participation

Electoral systems in the USA

Parties select candidates by means of primaries and caucuses, both for presidential and congressional elections, with the choice confirmed at national party conventions in the former case. Campaign finance laws and the extent to which the incumbency advantage — so significant in congressional elections (as noted in Topic 2) — also applies to presidential contests are notable areas of discussion. The role of the Electoral College can lead to the winner of the popular vote being denied the presidency, an outcome which has happened twice in the six elections between 2000 and 2020.

Practice questions ?

AO1 Knowledge and understanding

1 Explain the role of the following in the presidential election process:

   a   the constitutional requirements for a presidential candidate   **3 marks**

....

....

....

....

....

   b   the invisible primary   **3 marks**

....

....

....

....

....

2 a   What is the difference between primaries and caucuses?   **2 marks**

....

....

....

....

b What is the difference between closed primaries and open primaries? **1 mark**

  ....

  ....

3 Explain the role of national party conventions in the presidential election process. **3 marks**

  ....

  ....

  ....

  ....

  ....

AO2 Analysis

4 Explain the role of the Electoral College in presidential elections and why it is controversial. **4 marks**

Worked example

When casting their ballots in a presidential election, voters vote for electors to represent their state in the Electoral College. The Electoral College then formally selects the president on the first Monday after the second Wednesday in December. In all but two states the winner of the popular vote in a state takes all that state's electors, amounting in number to that state's combined total of senators and representatives. This system is controversial because the 'winner-takes-all' system in most states, together with overrepresentation of smaller states, can lead to the winner of the popular vote not winning the Electoral College and being denied the presidency, as happened in 2000 and 2016.

AO1 Clear and concise factual summary of how the Electoral College works.

AO2 Develops argument, explaining two features of the system that can lead to undemocratic outcomes.

AO1 Supports this point with two recent factual examples.

5 Study the table, which shows the outcome of elections since 1972 in which the incumbent president was running for re-election. Answer the questions that follow.

Election year	Incumbent	Challenger	Winner	Winning margins	
				Winning margins	ECVs
1972	Richard Nixon (R)	George McGovern (D)	Incumbent	23.2%	503
1976	Gerald Ford (R)	Jimmy Carter (D)	Challenger	2.1%	57
1980	Jimmy Carter (D)	Ronald Reagan (R)	Challenger	9.7%	440
1984	Ronald Reagan (R)	Walter Mondale (D)	Incumbent	18.2%	512
1992	George H. W. Bush (R)	Bill Clinton (D)	Challenger	5.6%	202
1996	Bill Clinton (D)	Bob Dole (R)	Incumbent	8.5%	220
2004	George W. Bush (R)	John Kerry (D)	Incumbent	2.4%	35
2012	Barack Obama (D)	Mitt Romney (R)	Incumbent	3.9%	126
2020	Donald Trump (R)	Joe Biden (D)	Challenger	4.4%	74

a   What percentage of incumbents have secured re-election in these elections?   1 mark

....

b   Are incumbent presidents more or less likely to secure re-election than
    incumbent congress(wo)men?   2 marks

....

....

c   Choose two of the following dates from the table: 1976, 1980, 1992 or 2020. What
    circumstances might explain why incumbent presidents lost in these years?   4 marks

....

....

....

....

AO3 Evaluation

6   There have been attempts to tackle the problem of the huge advantage enjoyed by
    well-financed candidates, by placing restrictions on how much money can be spent
    in elections and in what ways. Evaluate the success of the following measures
    to reform campaign finance: the Federal Elections Campaign Act (1971) and the
    Bipartisan Campaign Reform Act ('McCain-Feingold' Act) (2002).   5 marks

....

....

....

....

....

....

....

....

....

....

....

....

....

Key ideas and principles of the Democratic and Republican parties

In the twenty-first century, US political parties have become more ideologically coherent, and highly polarised: repeated studies have shown that the most conservative Democrat in the Senate is to the left of the most liberal Republican. Despite this polarisation and the growth in partisanship, both parties contain different factions with significant variations in beliefs and policies.

You should understand how the four factors of race, religion, gender and education are likely to influence voting patterns and why. You should study the influence of these factors on one presidential election campaign since 2000 — it is up to you which campaign you choose as your example.

Practice questions ?

AO1 Knowledge and understanding

7   What is meant by the following terms?

   a   Ideological coherence   1 mark

....

   b   Polarisation   1 mark

....

   c   Partisanship   1 mark

....

   d   Faction   1 mark

....

AO2 Analysis

8   In the table, summarise the typical positions the two parties adopt on the issues specified. **16 marks**

	Democrat	Republican
Social and moral issues		
Government intervention in the national economy		
Provision of social welfare		
Immigration		

9 Explain the differences between libertarians and social conservatives within
   the Republican Party.

   4 marks

....

....

....

....

....

....

....

....

....

AO3 Evaluation

10 Evaluate the significance of the division between progressives and centrists
   within the Democratic Party.

   5 marks

Worked example

Progressive or liberal Democrats call for measures to
safeguard the poorest and most vulnerable, such as Medicare
for all. Often critical of Wall Street and the banks, they demand
more regulation to protect consumers, while some describe
themselves as socialist. Moderate Democrats, however,
adopt a more pragmatic, ideologically centrist approach,
producing relatively modest reform measures, such as
Obamacare.

> AO1 Clear and concise summary of the priorities of progressive Democrats.

> AO1 Clear and concise summary of the priorities of centrist Democrats.

The significance of this division can be seen in Bernie Sanders'
tenacious campaigns for the Democratic nomination for
president in 2016 and in 2020, which prolonged the primary
campaigns and presented a disunited front to voters, and in the
emergence of 'The Squad', a group of young congresswomen
first elected in 2018 including Alexandria Ocasio-Cortez, who
attracted controversy by advocating left-wing policies, including
Medicare for all and the Green New Deal.

> AO3 Evaluates the significance of the division by citing two recent developments.

Yet the existence of these divisions did not prevent Joe Biden's
substantial victory over Donald Trump in the 2020 presidential
election, and his pursuit in office of surprisingly radical policies,
such as his $2 trillion infrastructure plan. This led to strong
support for Biden from both wings of the Democratic Party,
suggesting that the significance of the division was not as great
as it had previously seemed.

> AO3 Presents a counter-argument and concludes with a reasoned judgement on the issue.

Interest groups in the USA: their significance, resources, tactics and debates about their impact on democracy

Interest groups exert a powerful influence on US politics. They vary greatly in size, influence and purpose — some are institutional interest groups, such as the American Federation of Labor and Congress of Industrial Organizations (AFL–CIO), the largest federation of trade unions in the USA, while others are membership groups, such as the Sierra Club, an environmental pressure group. You need to study the influence, methods and power of at least one interest group, professional group or policy group. We looked at the NRA in Topic 2, and at the NAACP, BAMN, BLM and the ACLU in Topic 4. Any of these would be good examples, as well as those referred to in the questions in this section.

AO1 Knowledge and understanding

11 In the context of interest groups, define the following terms:

    a   Institutional interest groups   **1 mark**

....

....

    b   K Street   **1 mark**

....

....

AO2 Analysis

12 Explain how interest groups use amicus curiae briefs to further their cause.   **3 marks**

....

....

....

....

13 Analyse the aims and campaigning of the AFL–CIO.   **4 marks**

....

....

....

....

....

....

....

14 Explain how the separation of powers and federalism affect the way in which
   interest groups campaign for their cause.   **4 marks**

....

....

....

....

....

....

....

....

AO3 Evaluation

15 Evaluate the significance of political action committees (PACs) and Super PACs.   **5 marks**

....

....

....

....

....

....

....

....

....

....

....

....

....

....

Interpretations and debates of US democracy and participation

While Americans value their democratic tradition, the electoral process comes in for much criticism: the excessive length and expense of campaigns, the lack of effective controls on campaign finance, the influence of PACs and Super PACs, the undemocratic nature of the Electoral College, and the use of voter ID laws and redistricting to influence election outcomes.

AO3 Evaluation

16 In the table, evaluate the advantages and disadvantages of the specified features of the electoral process.

6 marks

	Advantages	Disadvantages
The Electoral College		
Voter ID laws		
Redistricting		

Paper 3 Section C

All of these exam-style questions require you to demonstrate AO1 (knowledge and understanding), AO2 (analysis) and AO3 (evaluation) in your answers.

1 Evaluate the extent to which attempts to regulate campaign finance have been unsuccessful. You must consider this view and the alternative to this view in a balanced way.

30 marks

40

Write a plan here, then use a separate sheet of paper to answer the question in full.

....

....

....

....

....

....

....

....

2   Evaluate the view that incumbency conveys an unfair and undemocratic advantage in both congressional and presidential elections. You must consider this view and the alternative to this view in a balanced way.   **30 marks**

Write a plan here, then use a separate sheet of paper to answer the question in full.

....

....

....

....

....

....

....

3   Evaluate the extent to which the main divisions within the Democratic Party and the Republican Party are significant. You must consider this view and the alternative to this view in a balanced way.   **30 marks**

Write a plan here, then use a separate sheet of paper to answer the question in full.

....

....

....

....

....

....

....

4   Evaluate the view that US presidential election campaigns are too long. You must consider this view and the alternative to this view in a balanced way.   **30 marks**

Write a plan here, then use a separate sheet of paper to answer the question in full.

....

....

....

....

....

....

....

5 Evaluate the extent to which race and gender influenced the outcome of the 2020 presidential election. You must consider this view and the alternative to this view in a balanced way.

30 marks

40

Write a plan here, then use a separate sheet of paper to answer the question in full.

....

....

....

....

....

....

....

6 Evaluate the view that the Electoral College should be abolished. You must consider this view and the alternative to this view in a balanced way.

30 marks

40

Write a plan here, then use a separate sheet of paper to answer the question in full.

....

....

....

....

....

....

....

7 Evaluate the view that interest groups are damaging to the democratic process. You must consider this view and the alternative to this view in a balanced way.

30 marks

40

Write a plan here, then use a separate sheet of paper to answer the question in full.

....

....

....

....

....

....

Topic 6 Comparative approaches

Theoretical approaches

Political scientists have developed three models for comparing systems of government: rational, cultural and structural. Each considers governmental systems being compared (in our case, the US and the UK systems) from different perspectives.

In the US option of Component 3 of the specification, **Section A** questions ask you to make a straightforward comparison of aspects of US and UK politics without necessarily mentioning the comparative theories, while in **Section B** questions, you must make the comparison referring to at least one comparative theory. In the exam, you will not be asked questions about the theories themselves, but you must use them as a means of comparing features of US and UK politics.

> **Practice questions ?**

AO1 Knowledge and understanding

1   Explain what is meant by rational theory.   2 marks

....

....

....

2   Explain what is meant by cultural theory.   2 marks

....

....

....

3   Explain what is meant by structural theory.   2 marks

....

....

....

AO2 Analysis

4   For each of the following examples, choose which of the three comparative theories you consider the most appropriate to refer to when comparing them, and briefly explain why:

   a   A study of the greater power and influence of pressure groups in the USA compared to those in the UK.   1 mark

....

....

....

b   A study of whether the shorter 2-year electoral cycle for the US House of Representatives leads to congress(wo)men being more concerned to be seen to be looking after the interests of the district they represent than UK MPs, who are elected on a cycle of up to 5 years.   1 mark

....

....

c   A comparison of the effects of the differing constitutional positions of the UK and US Supreme Courts.   1 mark

....

....

Similarities and differences in the UK and the USA

The systems of government of the USA and the UK share some broad underlying foundations, such as democratic accountability, and some practices, such as a first-past-the-post (FPTP) electoral system. But there are also some significant differences, most fundamentally the contrast between the USA's codified constitution and the UK's uncodified constitution.

As well as the nature of the two constitutions themselves, the following specific aspects are to be compared: federalism in the USA and devolution in the UK; Congress and Parliament; the offices of president and prime minister; the US and the UK Supreme Courts; how the rights of citizens of the USA and the UK are defined and protected by law; and democracy and participation in both countries, including parties and interest groups.

Practice questions

AO1 Knowledge and understanding

5   Complete the table, comparing key aspects of the US and the UK constitutions.   10 marks

	US Constitution	UK Constitution
Location of power		
Selection of head of government		
Constitutional court		
Defining rights of citizens		
Process for amendment of constitution		

6 Give two examples of UK Acts of Parliament since 1997 with constitutional significance, summarising how they changed the UK Constitution.   **4 marks**

....

....

....

....

....

....

7 Complete the table, comparing the constitutional position, powers and independence of the US and the UK Supreme Courts.   **10 marks**

	US Supreme Court	UK Supreme Court
Date and means of creation		
Constitutional position and entrenchment		
Power to strike down laws		
Appointment process		
Independence		
Example of recent significant case		

8 Complete the table, comparing key features of the US and the UK party systems.   10 marks

	US parties	UK parties
Principal parties		
'Third' parties		
Nature of parties in Congress/Commons		
Selection of candidates		
Nature of election campaigns		

AO2 Analysis

9 To what extent is the balance between the powers of the two houses different in the UK Parliament and the US Congress?   4 marks

....

....

....

....

....

....

....

....

....

10 How can cultural theory help to explain how US presidents and UK prime ministers try to put their policies into practice?

4 marks

Worked example

UK political parties have traditionally been more ideologically defined than the 'broad church' nature of US parties, a significant difference in political culture. This, together with a more rigid whipping system, has generally made it easier for UK prime ministers to implement their policies. As long as their party has a reasonable majority in the House of Commons, UK prime ministers are generally able to get their policies through parliament with few difficulties. Only when a prime minister has a perilously small majority (e.g. John Major, 1992–97) or no majority at all (e.g. Theresa May, 2017–19) are they likely to have serious difficulties persuading parliament to pass bills.

> AO1 Begins with a clear and concise summary of a key difference of political culture between the USA and the UK.

> AO2 Explains how political culture in the UK makes it easy for prime ministers to implement their policies.

In contrast, the looser nature of US parties has meant that presidents often have to work harder to persuade members of their own party in Congress to back their policies, as demonstrated by both the year-long struggle of President Obama to secure the passage of his flagship Affordable Care Act through Congress in 2009 and the failure of President Trump to repeal it 8 years later. In both cases, the same party controlled the presidency and both Houses of Congress, highlighting the major impact of this difference in political culture between the two countries.

> AO2 Signals comparison clearly by use of phrase such as 'in contrast…'.

> AO2 Explains how political culture in the USA can make it difficult for presidents to implement their policies.

> AO2 Concludes by reiterating what this tells us in terms of political cultural difference.

11 How can structural theory help to explain why US presidents sometimes have to work with a Congress controlled by a different party, a situation which is unlikely to happen to a UK prime minister?

5 marks

....

....

....

....

....

....

....

....

....

....

....

....

12 How can rational theory help to explain why US politicians generally prefer to be in the Senate rather than the House of Representatives, whereas UK politicians prefer the Commons to the Lords?

4 marks

....

....

....

....

....

....

....

....

....

....

Exam-style questions (?)

Paper 3 Section A

All of these exam-style questions require you to demonstrate AO1 (knowledge and understanding) and AO2 (analysis) in your answers. It is also essential to refer to both the US and the UK systems of government.

1 Examine the effects of the USA's codified constitution and the UK's uncodified constitution on the government of both countries.

12 marks

15

Write a plan here, then use a separate sheet of paper to answer the question in full.

....

....

....

....

....

....

....

....

....

2   Examine how the constitutional position of the state legislatures in the USA
    differs from that of the devolved assemblies in Scotland, Wales and
    Northern Ireland.   12 marks

Write a plan here, then use a separate sheet of paper to answer the question in full.

....

....

....

....

....

....

....

....

3   Examine the comparative strengths and weaknesses of the US Congress and the
    UK Parliament.   12 marks

Write a plan here, then use a separate sheet of paper to answer the question in full.

....

....

....

....

....

....

....

....

4   Examine the differences in the ways in which Congress can hold the US president
    to account and the ways in which the House of Commons can hold the
    UK prime minister to account.   12 marks

Write a plan here, then use a separate sheet of paper to answer the question in full.

....

....

....

....

....

....

5 Examine the effectiveness with which the rights of citizens are protected in the USA and the UK.

12 marks

15

Write a plan here, then use a separate sheet of paper to answer the question in full.

....

....

....

....

....

....

....

....

6 Examine the differences between the USA and the UK in the area of campaign finance and the funding of political parties.

12 marks

15

Write a plan here, then use a separate sheet of paper to answer the question in full.

....

....

....

....

....

....

....

....

7 Examine the reasons why US interest groups are more powerful than their UK counterparts.

12 marks

15

Write a plan here, then use a separate sheet of paper to answer the question in full.

....

....

....

....

....

....

....

Paper 3 Section B

All of these exam-style questions require you to demonstrate AO1 (knowledge and understanding) and AO2 (analysis) in your answers. It is also essential to refer to both the US and the UK systems of government and to make use of at least one comparative theory.

8   Analyse the differences in the flexibility of the constitution in the USA and in the UK. In your answer, you must consider the relevance of at least one comparative theory.

12 marks

Write a plan here, then use a separate sheet of paper to answer the question in full.

....

....

....

....

....

....

9   Analyse how their differing cultural and historical contexts account for the differences in the constitutions of the USA and the UK. In your answer, you must consider the relevance of at least one comparative theory.

12 marks

Write a plan here, then use a separate sheet of paper to answer the question in full.

....

....

....

....

....

....

10   Analyse the differences between the roles of UK MPs and US representatives and senators. In your answer, you must consider the relevance of at least one comparative theory.

12 marks

Write a plan here, then use a separate sheet of paper to answer the question in full.

....

....

....

....

....

....

11 Analyse the differences between the relationship of the US president and the UK prime minister with their cabinets. In your answer, you must consider the relevance of at least one comparative theory.

12 marks

15

Write a plan here, then use a separate sheet of paper to answer the question in full.

....

....

....

....

....

....

....

....

12 Analyse the differences in the powers of the US and the UK Supreme Courts. In your answer you must consider the relevance of at least one comparative theory.

12 marks

15

Write a plan here, then use a separate sheet of paper to answer the question in full.

....

....

....

....

....

....

....

13 Analyse the differences between the opportunities for participation in democracy and politics open to US and UK voters. In your answer you must consider the relevance of at least one comparative theory.

12 marks

15

Write a plan here, then use a separate sheet of paper to answer the question in full.

....

....

....

....

....

....

....